IT'S TIME TO EAT CARAMEL CANDY

It's Time to Eat CARAMEL CANDY

Walter the Educator

Silent King Books
A WhichHead Entertainment Imprint

Copyright © 2025 by Walter the Educator

All rights reserved. No part of this book may be reproduced in any manner whatsoever without written per- mission except in the case of brief quotations embodied in critical articles and reviews.

First Printing, 2024

Disclaimer

This book is a literary work; the story is not about specific persons, locations, situations, and/or circumstances unless mentioned in a historical context. Any resemblance to real persons, locations, situations, and/or circumstances is coincidental. This book is for entertainment and informational purposes only. The author and publisher offer this information without warranties expressed or implied. No matter the grounds, neither the author nor the publisher will be accountable for any losses, injuries, or other damages caused by the reader's use of this book. The use of this book acknowledges an understanding and acceptance of this disclaimer.

It's Time to Eat CARAMEL CANDY is a collectible early learning book by Walter the Educator suitable for all ages belonging to Walter the Educator's Time to Eat Book Series. Collect more books at WaltertheEducator.com

USE THE EXTRA SPACE TO TAKE NOTES AND DOCUMENT YOUR MEMORIES

CARAMEL CANDY

Hooray, hooray! It's time to see,

It's Time to Eat
Caramel Candy

A golden treat just made for me!

So soft and chewy, smooth and sweet,

Caramel candy, what a treat!

Wrapped up snug in shiny gold,

A tiny treasure to unfold.

Peel it back, oh, what a sight!

A caramel square so warm and bright.

Pop it in and take it slow,

Let it melt, don't bite, just know,

It's creamy, sticky, oh so fun,

A tasty treat for everyone!

Drizzle it on apples tall,

Or swirl it up, don't let it fall!

Dip your spoon and have a taste,

That caramel goodness won't go to waste!

It's Time to Eat
Caramel Candy

It stretches long and bends so neat,

A little piece is fun to eat.

Hold it tight, don't let it slip,

Or it might stick right to your lips!

Grandpa loves it, so does Sue,

Mom and Dad enjoy it too!

Golden, sticky, smooth and grand,

Caramel's loved in every land!

One by one, the pieces go,

Melting fast and sweetly slow.

Soft and buttery, rich and deep,

A caramel dream before we sleep!

Oops, sticky fingers, wipe them quick!

That caramel sure likes to stick!

But that's okay, it's worth the mess,

It's Time to Eat
Caramel Candy

It's still the treat we love the best!

Now the wrapper's empty, oh!

But don't be sad, we'll make more grow!

With sugar, butter, and some fun,

We'll cook up more for everyone!

So when you see that golden shine,

And smell the sweetness, oh, so fine,

You'll know it's time, come close, be handy,

It's Time to Eat
Caramel Candy

Time to eat caramel candy!

ABOUT THE CREATOR

Walter the Educator is one of the pseudonyms for Walter Anderson. Formally educated in Chemistry, Business, and Education, he is an educator, an author, a diverse entrepreneur, and he is the son of a disabled war veteran. "Walter the Educator" shares his time between educating and creating. He holds interests and owns several creative projects that entertain, enlighten, enhance, and educate, hoping to inspire and motivate you. Follow, find new works, and stay up to date with Walter the Educator™

at WaltertheEducator.com

www.ingramcontent.com/pod-product-compliance
Lightning Source LLC
LaVergne TN
LVHW052011060526
838201LV00059B/3964